Magic Spells
for
Lovers

igloo

This book is published by Igloo Books Ltd
Henson Way, Telford Way Industrial Estate
Kettering, Northants, NN16 8PX
First published in 2004
© Copyright Smiling Faces Limited and Sevens Design 2004
All rights reserved
Printed in India

info@igloo-books.com

Warning: Not suitable for children
under 3 years, due to choking hazard.

This Magic Spells book is for
lovers everywhere – would-be
lovers, new lovers, dissatisfied
lovers, not to mention lovers
in action! So if you want a little
more Magic in your love life,
take this book in your hand
and read aloud the Spells
inside. We can't guarantee
your success, but we wish you
lots of luck trying!

A Spell for
Everlasting Love

"I'd like a life that's really great
To share with the perfect mate.
So make me a love that will grow and grow,
Like a seed that you sow.
Make it last forever and ever,
Getting better whatsoever."

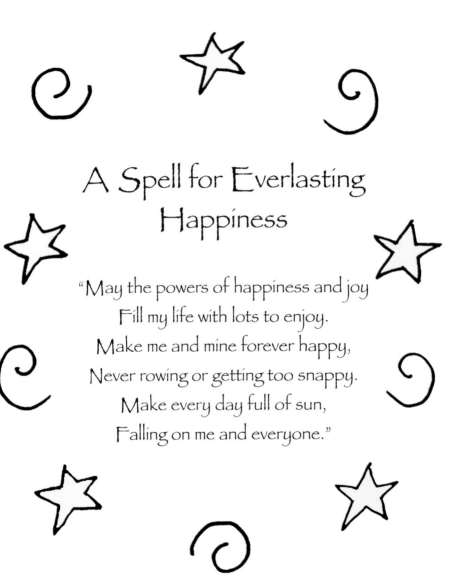

A Spell for Everlasting Happiness

"May the powers of happiness and joy
Fill my life with lots to enjoy.
Make me and mine forever happy,
Never rowing or getting too snappy.
Make every day full of sun,
Falling on me and everyone."

A Spell to
Get a Millionaire

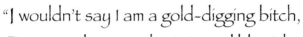

"I wouldn't say I am a gold-digging bitch,
But I need a man who is incredibly rich.
So make my life Magically Spellbound,
And create me a handsome man
With a few million pound.
Then I ask all that's Magical to hear my plea,
And make him fall in love with me."

A Spell to Make
You Irresistible

"With this Magic Spell I wish
To become a gorgeous irresistible dish,
Making everyone I meet
Fall in reverence at my feet.
Give me a well-toned body to flex,
So I can pull the opposite sex."

A Spell for
the Perfect Kiss

"As I've kissed many a frog,
And found no Prince worth a snog,
Find me a man who is gorgeous and fit,
Who's up for a snog and a bit of crumpet.
Make it moist,
Make it long,
And make him wear a tiny thong."

A Passion Spell

"A pinch of passion, a handful of lust,
Mixed up with some Fairy Dust,
To help create a day of romantic fun,
When we can show our love to everyone."

A Spell to Get
a Boyfriend

"I need some love and lots of attention,
Some TLC, and need I mention
Lots of fun both night and day,
And someone to cherish in every way."

A Spell to Get an Engagement Ring

"As I've found the man for me
I need him to get down on bended knee.
So I wish for roses and a bottle of wine,
With a romantic proposal as we dine.
Then make my new ring shine so bright,
That people think it's a new source of light."

A Romance Spell

"On this Valentine's Day,
I wish for a huge, beautiful bouquet.
Then perhaps as we dine
With fine food and expensive wine,
I can open a massive gift box,
Hiding a diamond ring inside
some Belgian chocs."

A Spell for the Perfect Body

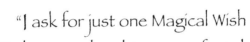

"I ask for just one Magical Wish
To become the ultimate perfect dish.
Give me unreceding hair and clear skin.
Give me a body that's muscly and thin.
Make me the object of others' desire,
No longer carrying an old spare tyre."

A Spell to
Make a Man Fitter

"My man has now let himself go,
Allowing his body to grow and grow.
So using the Magic in Fairy Wit,
Make him awake amazingly fit,
With massive pecs, a muscly back,
And the sexiest looking six-pack."

A Spell for Revenge
on a Love Rat

"I've discovered my man has cheated on me,
So all that's Magic hear my plea.
Make his willy only rise
When he's around other guys,
So all his days are filled with fear,
As he starts to wonder if he's turned queer."

A Spell to
Let a Bloke
Down Gently

"This guy I've met is kind of 'nice',
But doesn't possess any kind of spice.
In fact I'd say he's rather dull,
Not gorgeous or cute or masterful.
But I wish to let him down slow,
And not hurt his 'nice' tender ego.
So all that's Magic hear my plea,
And let him forget he ever met me."

A Fantasy Spell

"If I only had one special Wish to use,
Then I know what I would choose
To make my fantasy come true,
With no guilt added to make me rue.
So give me a couple of gorgeous twins,
With cute bums and sexy grins."

A Spell to Get
the Perfect Woman

"Shallow I am, shallow I be.
Help me find the perfect woman for me.
She should have a thin waist and huge breasts,
And with a stunning face be magically blessed.
Also make her laugh at all my jokes,
And come boozing like one of the blokes.
But make her never whinge or whine
Like all women do, given time."

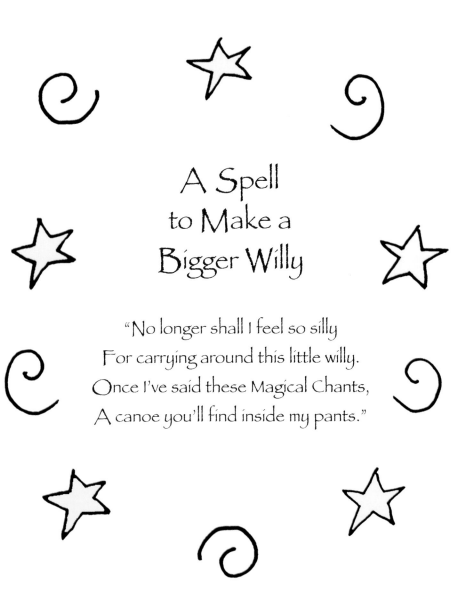

A Spell to Make a Bigger Willy

"No longer shall I feel so silly
For carrying around this little willy.
Once I've said these Magical Chants,
A canoe you'll find inside my pants."

A Spell to Turn a Man into a Toad

"My man treats me really bad,
And is an absolute sexist cad.
In order to get my own back
I'd like to turn him into a Natterjack.
So I call upon the Magic in this rhyme
To turn him into a toad, the rotten swine."

A Dear John Spell

"As I am useless at dumping men,
I thought I'd write him with my pen.
But as I can't think of what to say
I ask this Spell to guide my way.
I want to tell him that we're through,
So I can find someone exciting and new."

A Spell to Swap a Bloke

"I want to trade in my guy,
And give a new one a three-month try.
So swap my lazy old man
For one with muscles and a tan.
Make him hunky, make him cute,
And make him have loads of loot."

A Spell to Improve
Your Sex Life

"My sex life is now very sad,
And goes from dull to extremely bad.
So I call on the powers of debauchery
To make my life more of an orgy.
I'd like to swing from the chandelier,
And use with style my God-given gear."

A Spell to Make You Look Sexy

"Next time I wear sexy underwear,
I want my man to really stare.
Instead of flesh hanging over my panty line
I wish to look completely divine.
No more ripples,
No more spare tyre –
Just a figure to really admire."

A Spell to
Stop a Guy Calling

"My phone is forever ringing off the hook,
Because of a guy who's completely mistook.
He thinks I'm interested in his body,
And wants me to be his bit of totty.
So with the Magic in this Spell,
Make him understand the words 'Go to Hell'."

A Spell to Dump a Bloke

"As I'm sick of my present bloke,
Because he's turned into a bit of a joke,
With the help of the Magic here,
I wish to make him disappear.
No creeping phone call,
No writing 'Dear John'.
Just a fella who is suddenly gone."

A Spell to Understand Women

"My woman says I don't understand her,
And instead the television I prefer.
So help me get inside her mind,
But protect me from some of what I might find.
So next time she's banging on at me,
I can nod my head and totally agree."

A Spell for a
Special Wedding

"We call upon the Wedding Dove
To make our lives full of love.
Make us lucky,
Make us happy,
Help us to never get too snappy.
Ensure we last for evermore,
Through good and bad and love and war.
Make every day feel brand new,
And make the sex-life fantastic too."

A Spell for a Great Honeymoon

"I'm looking forward to my honeymoon night,
But I'm feeling worried and a bit uptight.
So I ask the power in this Spell
To keep me performing extremely well.
And if I can make the earth move,
I'm sure my partner will really approve."

A Spell for a
Special Anniversary

"Now we've reached that time of year
When we celebrate what means so dear.
We ask for our time ahead
To be as wonderful as the day we wed.
Keep us happy and always loving.
Keep us listening and truly giving.
Make our days ahead so swell,
And keep the sex great as well."

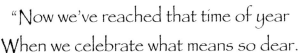